DRUM LEGENDS ALPHABET

Words by Robin Feiner

A is for **A**rt Blakey. This legend made his name in big band jazz in the 1940s before playing bebop alongside the great Dizzy Gillespie, Charlie Parker and Thelonious Monk. Later, his own band, Art Blakey and the Jazz Messengers, became known for supporting and encouraging young talent.

B is for Cindy **B**lackman Santana. As Lenny Kravitz's go-to session player for more than 18 years, Cindy's playing style is as cool as it is powerful. She also plays Latin rock alongside husband and guitar legend Carlos Santana. Two legends in one family!

Cc

C is for Stewart Copeland. One of the most revered drummers of the modern era, The Police drummer plays a very intricate style of fusion, pop and reggae rhythms. He's also composed music for movie soundtracks and been inducted into multiple Halls of Fame.

D is for **D**ave Grohl. The young David became a Goliath when he brought his heavy, hurricane style and long hair to grunge gods, Nirvana. He would later form UFO-loving legends the Foo Fighters, be inducted into the Rock and Roll Hall of Fame, and win 16 Grammys. He has been described as one of the most influential musicians of the past 20 years!

E is for Elvin Jones. Watching the circus bands that came to town, a young Elvin discovered his love of drums and joined his high school marching band. Following his dream to New York City, he would play alongside jazz legends like John Coltrane and Miles Davis.

F is for Mick **F**leetwood. Despite being the namesake of classic rockers Fleetwood Mac, Mick's style was never over-the-top or showy. Instead, he played with perfect time-keeping and a subtlety that let the big personalities shine. Fans will always remember his work in 'Tusk.'

G is for **G**inger Baker. With a polyrhythmic drumming style as wild as his personality, he often challenged guitarist Eric Clapton to match his moves, which made their rock group, Cream, huge and heavy. He would later look to Africa for drumming's roots to perform alongside Afro-beat drummer Tony Allen.

Hh

H is for **H**al Blaine.
As drummer of session legends
The Wrecking Crew, Blaine
would become one of the
most recorded drummers in
history! He played with The
Beach Boys and Elvis Presley,
and also created the iconic
and often imitated beat on
The Ronettes' 'Be My Baby.'
Boom boom-boom bap.

I is for Ian Paice.
Known for his speed, power and technique, Paice was instrumental in elevating Deep Purple to the heavy metal pioneers they became. As an inductee of both the Rock and Roll, and Modern Drummer's Halls of Fame, he's a certified legend!

J is for **J**ohn Bonham.
He made his indelible mark
on rock and roll as the
drummer of Led Zeppelin.
It all started with 'Good Times
Bad Times.' Then came the
drum solo in 'Moby Dick'
and everything after. Many
believe Bonham to be the
greatest rock drummer
of all time.

K is for **K**aren Carpenter. With a flowing style, both intricate and precise, Karen was a jazz drummer by trade and a singer by fame. Energetic and playful, she seemed never happier than when performing onstage behind the kit with her band. A legend gone too soon.

L is for Tommy **L**ee.
This tattooed, bombastic
showman of glam rock band
Mötley Crüe, plays loud and
lives louder, putting his drum
kit in cages and even on
roller coasters during concerts!
The way he hit his drums,
you'd think he hated them
as much as he hated hotel
TV sets!

M is for Keith **M**oon.
The Who's chaotic Keith Moon was the original Rock Star. His hyper style, using heavy double kick pedals and rolling tom fills, was equal parts heavy rock and jazz. He inspired so many great drummers who came after him, including Animal from The Muppets!

N is for **N**eil Peart. Known to fans as The Professor, this virtuoso drummer led his Canadian prog-rock group, Rush, through complicated rhythms and off-kilter time-signatures. His mind-blowing tracks are some of the most rehearsed by drum students around the world.

Oo

O is for Omar Hakim.
A session drummer with A-list rock and pop musicians, Hakim's clean and crisp, funky beats have filled dance floors for Madonna, David Bowie and Daft Punk, and backed jazz cats like Miles Davis and Roy Ayers. Playing since he was just five years old, Hakim proves you're never too young for the drums!

P is for **P**hil Collins. Whether he played with 70s rock band, Genesis, or as a solo artist, Collins always dazzled behind both mic and kit. Of course, his greatest gift to air-drummers around the world will forever be three minutes and 40 seconds into 'In the Air Tonight' for his heavily anticipated, gorilla-sized drum fill!

Q is for **Q**ueen of Percussion: Sheila E. A child prodigy in a drumming family, it was no surprise when Sheila Escovedo was hired as Prince's drummer and musical director. As the Queen of Percussion, she would go on to release her own albums, and record with Beyoncé, Hans Zimmer and Cyndi Lauper. Give the drummer some!

R is for Buddy Rich. Described by his own hero, Gene Krupa, as the "greatest drummer to have ever drawn breath," Buddy is a true legend. From his rapid fire hi-hats to his polyrhythmic snare, he was super technical, and had the power to match.

S is for Ringo **S**tarr. Putting the beat in The Beatles, this legendary lefty was universally praised for his innovation and feel. It's hard to imagine the Beatles' songs without his swampy, psychedelic style of loose hi-hat and ramshackle drum. Ringo truly was a star on the kit.

T is for Moe Tucker.
With a snare, two toms
and an upturned bass drum,
Maureen 'Moe' Tucker played
standing up. And instead
of using drum sticks, she
pounded marching mallets!
Her minimalist, time-keeper
approach to playing helped
position Velvet Underground
as the forebearers of the
punk rock movement!

U is for Lars Ulrich.
Fast and ferocious, this
metal-head transformed
his garage band into one
of the biggest in the world
when he turned the bass
drum into a stampede of
elephants! Forty years later,
Metallica is still a force
to be reckoned with.
Absolute legends.

V is for Alex **V**an Halen. Naming your band after yourself is a big call, but Alex and his guitarist brother Eddie, had the chops to back it up. Van Halen became stadium rock gods, and Alex's flamboyant showmanship showed up in huge drum solos on hits like 'Panama,' 'Jump' and 'Why Can't This Be Love.'

W is for Charlie **W**atts. Although he's been the backbone of the most enduring rock and roll band for nearly 60 years, his personal tastes actually lie in jazz. He brings not only sartorial style, but an effortless cool and swinging swagger to the Rolling Stones' iconic brand of rhythm and blues. A true living legend.

X is for Ma**x** Roach.
As one of the pioneers of bebop jazz, Roach is considered one of the most important drummers in history! A Hall of Famer, this old dog kept learning new tricks, innovating with improvized jazz and collaborating with dancers and hip hoppers well into his 70s. So cool!

Y is for Yoshimi P-We. She's been the driving beat behind Japanese noise punk legends, Boredoms, since 1986, simultaneously singing and sampling her way through the chaos. She's toured and collaborated with many experimental musicians, and is the namesake of The Flaming Lips album, 'Yoshimi Battles the Pink Robots!'

Z is for Joseph 'Zigaboo' Modeliste. At the center of funk band, The Meters, is New Orleans legend 'Ziggy,' who plays like an unconventional metronome. His sharp funk shows that the empty spaces between the beats are as important as the beats themselves. He has been a huge inspiration, constantly re-invented via hip hop sampling.

The ever-expanding legendary library

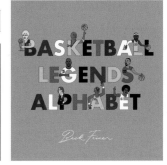

EXPLORE THESE LEGENDARY ALPHABETS & MORE AT WWW.ALPHABETLEGENDS.COM

DRUM LEGENDS ALPHABET
www.alphabetlegends.com

Published by Alphabet Legends Pty Ltd in 2021
Created by Beck Feiner
Copyright © Alphabet Legends Pty Ltd 2021

9780648962885

Printed and bound in China.

ALPHABET LEGENDS